The Geese in Logic

poetry by

Ann Douglas

The author gratefully acknowledges the following where some of these poems first appeared:
The Colorado Review, "Crow in Ordinary Flashback"; *Cake*, "The Orchards"; *Antiphon*, "The Geese in Logic"; *The Meadowland Review*, "Snow Pack"; *The Grey Sparrow Journal*, "Homestead", "Harvest Photograph"; *London Grip* "Ledger"; *Solstice,* "Hidden Valley"; *Women's Voices for Change,* "Hound Point"; *Boston Poetry Magazine*, "Moths", "Doubly Guided", "New Lands, East, West", "Kestrel Ridge", "Apple Orchards Hung with Foil Deflectors"; *Fifth Wednesday Journal*, "Lordosis"; *Agave Magazine*, "Abandoned Orchard."

Cover image: Orchards II (2013) "Apple Orchard: from "Wisdom of Trees" series by Donald Saaf, used with permission.

ISBN: 978-0-9985463-9-1
LCCN: 2017960542

FIRST EDITION

Published by
Ravenna Press
(ravennapress.com)

Recovering Apple Orchard

East Cascades

Table of Contents

I
Crow in Ordinary Flashback : 3
Bounty : 4
The Geese in Logic : 6
Genealogical Sifts : 11
West of the Scablands : 13
Amor Fati : 17
Quartz : 18
Prospect Butte : 20
Iron River : 22
Hound Point : 24
Kingston Blacks : 25

II
Field with Gate : 29
No Different : 31
Snow Pack : 35
Lordosis : 36
Bitch : 39
Kestrel Ridge : 41
New Lands, East, West : 43
Doubly Guided : 47
Trees Hung with Foil Deflectors : 48

III
Entering the Valley Downstream : 53
A Reserved Attitude, Perhaps Victorian : 61
Delphinium, Speaking from the Frontier : 62

Promise : 64
Seven Candles : 66
Cutting to the Lateral : 67
Apex : 69
Speckled Fritillaries : 70
Delphinium Speaks with Larkspur : 73
Larkspur Addressing Delphinium: 75
Delphinium/ Larkspur : 76
Summer Evening : 77
Red-Tail Basin : 79
Wide Angle : 83
Throat : 85
Ledger : 86
Cellar : 88

IV

Alibi Pass : 93
Curve : 94
Under Birdwoman Glacier : 96
Inside the Horizon : 98
Skew : 99
Weathered Shed : 100
Arial Weave : 101
Ditch : 102
Season of Corn Snow : 104
Caterpillars : 105
Reveille : 106

About the Author

I

Crow in Ordinary Flashback

Graying the fence—a crow's
shadow pecking
shadow, and
the chokecherry's—

I'm aware of the cost adding-up
every time I see it again.

Flat wings
flexing on plaster.

To watch my tender abstraction
—so extended, so widening—

turn on me—
sheer as an amethyst day—

I'm not seeing the tiny con,

that might-as-well-be
maggot.
No more than a haiku.
Or banging shutter.

Bounty

We liked the blood
in the mouth of qualification.

It was like owning
land.
      A horizon of hills absorbed
the hematite bloom of sundown

indifferently.
To be viewed
           took no effort
of their own. Their splendor
survived

like unfound copper
within.
      Remember?

Remember treasure, our own real treasure, buried
from the wrecked Ninabella,
doubloons and trinkets

wrapped in beeswax,
the Spanish chest
swum ashore. Like children we knew
the headland
peat, in which it was hidden

and then to warn the Indians—
topped with a freshly killed

slave. Only a few
gray clumps of crust remain

for the digging,
yours and mine, our commitment
with pails and plastic shovels,

deepening a bounty,
or loyal little husk of suchlike,
        soon enough empty of us.

The Geese in Logic

1 Geese

Innocence, the tender
unpacking
              of white clouds
our god sends us,
rolling east, gathering against
the planet's turn, to soften

and distract us—
                  shadowing
hillsides, crossing fields,
answering iron,
a body's
model of possession.

Between keeping us
and losing us,
between us—
              it is He
who grants
and withholds,
              doles
and doesn't.
What sticky innocence falls
for this

and starry-eyed, keeps choosing it?
I hear the calls
axiomatic
          of His most

singular, chipped flint
of straight
                skim close to the earth.

From His left hand, the geese
streak for His right
as by the force of his own
reflection
south, north.

They resist gravity
back and forth,
before and after.

  2 Residents

What is it He wants?
pulling us
away from the motherly forgone
conclusion—
and breaking our rough
pioneering hearts

the youngest stumbling along behind,
gripping her memory
of before.

  3 Rock

Because we know the Valley
can't be seen
as green in May
fruitful in autumn

without His discipline,
we strain to please Him.

Stretching our backs,
we inhale the monopoly
before us,
            the wholesome view
that sweeps the stars with winter
coming—
            the mountains,
granite blue, suggestive
of harvest, alfalfa baled, honey—darker
than any we've ever known,

and so sweet,
it'll burn the hair off
any latency
of a grief
            sitting alone
on a field rock.

    4 Pyramid Point

Sometimes flight, sometimes twilight.
They broker the changes:

ponderosas bathing in sunset,
plating the river

persimmon then dark
getting darker, maternal

as the back of her coat
turning away, receding.
Only God is permanent.

It is His will
that guides us
from the top needle of Pyramid Point

where light focuses the end
of our long valley in the mirroring
white of its glacier.

  5 High Water

How could she?
I stare at the river,
weakened by sorrow:

damn memory,
                    poor secondary
sadness of an after-thought.

I'm told, move fast enough
you'll forget.

I stall among the stones
on the beach.
                    A child is still a ghost
too dumb-struck

to fasten to the thrill of the river,
its fogs clearing by noon.

6 Photograph

The afternoon sun shines low
on the old ponderosas.
I pull over to park by the river.

But perhaps—He won't notice
if I make this once
of the slippery water, pumpkin
red,
     a postponement.

The apposite and fitting and emptying
accompanying
          current
under the trees and projection—a freeze,
once—
     everything and all
my heart,
as much as it can hold.

Genealogical Sifts

How intimate an idea
can be, naked,
obloid
in its nest. It grew
gave birth.

Wanting to rub up
against it, the next

daughter notion—inviting air and
want
        to cross on a plain—

Don't ask.
It's the deer who supply action,

A yearling demonstrates—
lipping a leaf from the snow pack,
staring back, chewing
silently.

But back to the idea in its state, already slapped
into being. How
can the dazed move, it asks

except in circles. How
to recognize one's self except forward.
A person calling out—

though they were there all the while, summits
exhaling moons

modeling this vantage and that,

or the jets and rubies of bantams
that shitting, melt the snow.

West of the Scablands

1 The Orchards

On these sandy bench-lands
stacked toward the hills
hope became capital,

exchange making visible
the earth's forward conveyance.

Like watching apples form in trees.

Yellow moons waxing
from the window, punctured
the brown haze of spinning silicates.
Grass leaned windward.
The rifle we unearthed, we used,
muzzle still loaded, front sight
a penny.

2 In the Interim

Backhoes revolving
blandly in place—
                    Dozers uprooting
and clearing the stumps:

an old orchard
can be razed in a week
stacked, burned.

Open dirt invites the sun to shine.

3 Homestead

Walk with me through June
down the aisles, drinking coffee.

Morning sunshine straight as rebar
slants from the summit.
Steaming beams fence the orchard.

Don't tell me they aren't omens
of good fortune.

Sweat: glory.
We hear the two sing,

one to another—
across the straightened steppes.

Who cares that I talk to the dead,
checking for rust,
examining the leaves for bud-sites.

4 Bare Roots

North covering our backs
we're learning
to assess
            the horizon before us,
its westerly swerve,
as green
            becoming yellow,
the season tips

toward depletion, toward the basaltic
in distance, its chiaroscuros
in autumn,

         and closer to
God—
     Such is a child's trust,
presuming
we don't impose.

   5 Due Zenith

Born to a gravitational field,
our notions
couldn't escape

         the earth's
magnetic return. Up, down: red hot
they pushed their glassy
skins,
     expanding to marvel
at their reach, and whorl

before slumping
through the likewise
charged climate—

Great predications
pulled home,
         hardened
into the landscape
steeped in blue burning leaves.

6 Early Drops

Hot afternoons, exhaustion
drives us to the trees,
the underside
                 tang
of dimension, damask

of shade. Between limb and ground,
July's falls
simmer with rust and vinegar.
Wasps dig through foam.

Yet this spent,
winter can't worry us.
We can't be spurred
can't remember
can't imagine below zero
anymore, anywhere,
ever in fact, again.

Amor Fati

It was an enormous maple
more like a shrub
grown into a seventy-foot tree.

We characterized such display
in terms of character.

Branches stretched above as roots
spread below,
leaving the heart exposed.

Or rather, we believed a story comes true
by ending

full-circle, protecting
the center
and a center's expansion. The night's
details twinkled in the snow
of hardboiled stars.

Old homestead shade tree near
the predictable Wilson rose,
or Vitruvian Man reaching up through pavement.

While all the while earth
and hurl: theirs
was the crucial relationship.

Quartz

I'd like to speak from inside the spar
as its walls formalize.

Accusation draws on story.

So many g-forces later I'm here to report

how the spar cuts both sides

of ten. Trapped flash—in, and

glassy arriving radiance flung—
out. No more

windy unshingling
roof otherwise.

No balancing point of judicious
accountings and strenuous teeter.

I prefer to reign
bard-like—
an edict or temple or sob

of glory so weighty and compact and metamorphosed
as to send all believers
with the hills
            on vacation.

Even the permanence

of a French cathedral secretly
subversively,
                    would out-challenge
God.
Consider the steeple.

As if plotted, gravity achieved in stone
pairs with air

and wins.
You could say at this juncture, I am
home
in a point solar-charged.
Time stops,

may stop, but is not eliminated. Watch me
sting the sill with a glow.

Prospect Butte

1 Planting Alfalfa

Seeing the green and gold of these fields
cut from the desert
moved God.
               He wept—

until His attention drifted,
and gravity failed.

It was a mistake, He argued,
that the children spilled.

2 Following the Catastrophe

Ever after, God
promised to focus His energy
in a straight, task-bearing line
completing each moment step by step
towards

the beauty of a unified
belief in Him as the world
trailed behind.
               No more
drunken stumbling.
No loose ends, nor shall
You indulge in rogue
poly-chronologies,
               He chided Himself—

Dropping His shadow
behind the shed, it was only privately
that Our God allowed
Himself visions of the forests
through smoke.

He dreamed thickly
of the earth
swallowing down
rivers again, to forget
the wayward diurnal give and vast
countering
retraction of the oceans' pull again.

Iron River

Red the red
wheelbarrow mounded
with cuttings, and straight
the trunks of outlying
conifers.
      Here and there to the open view
we added a fencepost,
grounding it to yearning.

Who can forget
the initiating
burst of acid into song,

or forget its rules,

prostration to motion.

So what
if we did invite those wooden handles to splinter
our hands.
      Easier that way

to dream, minding
the spin of a tool's
directive

flicking ahead
—as it should—
toward the bluebirds' return,
blood caked to eggs, blossoming
peas.

Dreaming through winter,
lumber of lumber and summer dust, the rose
in smoke, in ash
under heavy down snows.

Hound Point

When the moon came up
it was ours.

         Sad to say, it bothered me
that anyone else
could see it otherwise,
                  you know, as theirs
down in California,
in photographs, or on pilgrimages
with walking sticks
             inside painted
jars from China.

Kingston Blacks

Friends joined us, thinning the apples.
In the bump and wagony years
seasons gained new weight.

Success as red and gold
held aloft: ornament
on the ear of heaven.
Was He listening?

and would He, like daylight
intervene, choose between us, shining on each—
intimates to
                our perpetuating—constant
and driving
need—

some shaking limbs,
some crating the fall for cider.

We pinned His word
to our hearts
like a logo:
                a zigzag
clip of lightning.

Driving posts or stretching wire—

People harvesting the draws.

How to contain such sweetness?

Yet, as we turned to ask
Him—

                it was fortune
that spun the miniscule *if*
into jet streams.

Fortune-by-foot-or-wing, but *fleet*
enough to do so invisibly, bent
alongside us, securing
our will to His

and His to fruition, a bludgeoning—
I mean burgeoning—fruition but still fruition.

We baled then stacked hay.

It made sense
to me—
                as numbers
                                gained velocity, their own

expediency,

omniscience, ease of
tilt and
omnipotence, that looking down

He would rely
                on axis
and core
as if to navigate
with a thumb
the spin
of the earth inversely.
Fortune was a game

no matter what is said.
Private as credit.

II

Field with Gate

Across the field, the cattle gate
sweeps heavily open—

clicks behind.
Defeating the rain

a stove fills the kitchen with cloves.
We have grown rich. On the plaster,
places and people
are hung
             with an inwardness
that's outward—
                        images
of a lake
before the earthquake—
faces full of broad likenesses—

God's nonplussed
from His place across the table.

He sees us laughing, tipping back our chairs.
What were we thinking?

inviting the Dictator
home—robed, staffed, original

dissolutionist.
                        He
taps His foot under the chair,
where the sole thins

the magenta carpeting, its green wool, felted indigos,
grasses and sagebrush.

Against what, God
and gravity might argue, fate
or history, Is our earth so rapidly hurling?

No Different

1 Tiger Swallowtail

No different from a butterfly—
(wings or partitions or sectors)
perch

from flux—of wind, flutter: an address

sites itself in the shift

like straw taking on
October,
a stop on the tip, swallowtail
then air
          as air sculpts
and is resculpted
so that He became the best response

to attachment

and would carry form
in toto forward

eryngium-loaded,
effulgence needing a home.

What context can do,
pinching the wing. The moment
bermed,
timbered, windowed, 270.

In such a place
missing's old horror, child's
sickness—could take
a breath,
          a dandelion
pillow, willow branch
bed.

   2 Winter

The valley is a den—
bower
or spot on a graph out of which
He's gone
either up, or ahead,
He who dines with angels.

That's archangel
to you.

Numeral.
Compared to infinity,
you huddle
in your calorie with everyone else's.

God knows your natural devotion.
He sees that numbers serve.

All He need do
is point
to a void, and you believe
in the cold.
He lifts His finger, frosting

the rivers until tinkling,
and the angels laugh
over His shoulder.

3 Cabin near Gravity

How silently our cabin,
with its sweated
gabion

gateposts, honors Him by replacement.

Built of the tight
pulp of old fir drained
of sound, the frame balances itself
handsomely.
                        Everyone agrees
the structure is solid.
Good use of materials.
Reinforced concrete, steel joists, beams, they
cradle the skull-like vault
that across a kingdom
melts its walls
as belief sets in, applying its method,
a winnowing one,
the one.

4 Homestead Yarrow

To materialize
even a new type
of yarrow: that was the all
time existed for.

And on this, time took both a cool
and straight line:

first,
then absolute

then order.
With strategy
as with purpose, it
evolved, accrued
                    density: whole
complexities,
ecologies from which
one loss
could be understood
as no different than total.

Snow-pack

Snow slips
the rises
deepens roadsides,
rots.

Gravity's adipose
slide—fat dame on the tracks

or it could be a man
rather sinuously

slung.
            Yes, yes

it's dwindling
snow but across the back slope
why drag

on the world so entreatingly

winters later, long into

the slick skull-pan of
a lesson
            and it in return
bucking back.

Lordosis

1

Transfixed.
          I confess
that I've never escaped my human
window
          of lordosis,
no matter my age,
never before, thought to
anymore than my sisters did
or mother.
          Beholding
the dusk presenting itself low
to the world, pink filling
the yard, I colluded. I didn't
break away, much less, finally quit.

The stars lasted till just after dawn.

By that kind of span—
like living
in a cottage, we blamed
our mother as she'd blamed hers.

Even the towering clump of a city
or slow-motion desert was a sill
to restrain us here, inviting
more of the same.

As our own mother
focused her sights to meet
spangles from elsewhere,

and abandoned us,
we learned to pine,

　　　　　　　　　using our songs
to replace her.

2

Watching her fill
and empty, we bulged and hollowed
as well—received,
lost. Our flat bodies
so calm at sea
were pulled to the sand,
constituted,
deflated.

Gravity abetted
the play with undertow. What
could I do?
　　　　　There was logic
in the spell and suck
of its progression.

3

Morning pushed against
darkness—
Dew slipped down glass, seeking sea-level.
I cultivated the spectacle
of my desertion

so well, I banked there,
filling out forms at various sites
along with my sisters.

Anyone could spot us
though no one said so.

    4

Come! And
come-back! We called.
                  Our shill
from the rocks, picked up in the spray,
twisted into melody.
Waves reached for the notes.

Or when our mother, testing the wind, looked up—
the sky
blue as bouquets of iris
                        left at the door—
that's all she heard:
a rippling

tin-foil roar
as the bay stunned
the shore.
           Suitors, interests

fell off,

but from then on
we understood them. The plaintive,
counting
           outside world—would be stranded
unconsummated—
extinct—unless we succumbed.

Bitch

A bitch senses under her padded
paws, the earth
as it fattens
so verdantly, it pulsates.

Between animal and core,
the message
of the Valley is, Continue—
It is up to her, lifting her tail

on finding a warm pocket,
then tucking her flank round her
to express the betrayals
the new perform
on the formers

like snow
pulling down leaves and brown apples.

When she keens from Mt. Crag
a listener knows, this is not Paradise.

Climbing later
                out of
her den to greet the spring, she sees it
swell the steppe-lands again,
bringing in bluebirds,
waking wild celery.
She stretches her hindquarters after chewing live
        rabbit.

Without changes, the Honey Crisps,
Pink Ladies, Chisel Jerseys
would be simplified

to a straight, unending, predictable
line. Think of it.

No gambler would lose.
Tomatoes, bougainvillea, their yield
never rest.

Kestrel Ridge

Naturally, God is in charge.
Sometimes, however, when gravity
gets out of hand,
by which I mean, possessive
like a map
privileging itself—
doesn't it seem right
that God should intervene.
Stopping time
gives the earth like a mother
of children, a lift.

When everything loses
on par, and with the warehouse cleared,

there are no contingencies,
no necessary exits.

For awhile we are dead.

Allow me to add, this is His
understanding, not mine,
nor the quails'
        from the sound of them.
To plant our faith in the rush—

then have it reversed
against itself
        and back to Him—
as from streaking horsetails to heaven

either way—
though we've worked this hard—
we still have no traction.

New Lands, East, West

That's why we have rules
my friend, T, explains. Bacteria

moves quicker
                            than we can
into the future.

About fires, she says, smoldering
make excellent kindling.

I could have protected them.
I could have assumed an earlier
regret—
            Lightning
from nowhere—could have inspired in me
prayer.

From a swirl
of unstable heat, the fire volleyed downriver
toward us.

*How could you
not see this as war?*

is what I imagine she'd say
if she weren't already so busy—
(an activist even in my head.)

This is a friend who can direct convoys.
She hoists drums and 50# packs,
boards the helicopter.

What a vision
to see one's house among houses outlined
in cherry

warping the moon as it bores
through twilight to report back,
rock to void.

Such compression on community
like oxygen
spins a centrifugal
model of command
                    across a vacuum
roaring
many-armed, centered
like a tilting pinwheel.

Winding sirens
shriek up Edgecliff toward the smoking trenches—

I could have danced—
I could have joined our women
bare breasted, ribbons flying
round and round the Maypole
each spring.

Cosmic monoxide and sparks, the fires,
chest against chest,
meet like two bucks clacking headgear.
Eventually as God's ardor
met His match, He is soothed.

Only a witch,

our sister to flame
would distrust prevailing wisdom.

In matters of fire-fighting,
of investment
and protection,

history was taking
itself seriously,
                    whose favored state

keeps us breathing.
You can imagine its importance here. A breath
for seven
                    scarves, three
from four, and one, I imagine, the instant

reckoned from a pack,
exits outright

like sparks spit from a whining circular saw
as it cuts through cottonwood.

God manages
though without enough crews.

Afterwards, we sift the creek stones
round as mushrooms large to small

that marked the drives off Jumpers Bluff.
It turns out granite burns.

Then what did history expect for its part
fused to God like a comet's tail

if not pay?
            It stretched
in one direction,
pared to the Gulf Stream,
                        ready
for that thing like due—
no, no,
witch, like gratitude.

Doubly Guided

An apple, and parallel
being—its value

its yield
set themselves up
in the acids of summer

as earlier
in pink clouds
then white haze,

they sped through the visibilities
of conversion. So
crops bear, must bear, must
compete, key
word—compete—straining ahead
for all of us.

Trees Hung with Foil Deflectors

The idea formed,
had formed—prefab

that symmetry like law
like balance

would knit us together.

Geese
met Earth's curve and
bent. Honking
ripped the air, lifted rivers—
rapids and flew them. Truth presided, the one
thriving on contest

within accord.
Loose azures
heavenly enough

to recruit the McCalmon
peak blue, flash blue.

No one was meant
to be by the glare of the seen, un.

Such was not the intention.
God likes

rooms within chambers, forms
within forms, His
form.

But luck

needs no self, no
God's warty right hand.

Luck just happens
in the old aristocratic sense,

rising carelessly
from some hidden left hand,
presumptive of a perfect southern exposure.

When it comes to success
what don't the dead get?

III

Entering the Valley Downstream

* New Orchard

The sun favors us
on the back side of Titans' Bells.

We accept our radiance head-on.

By rock, by fusion, by up-thrust
granite packing
veins of iron, silver—God.

Though He hides His provisos.
When watered too early, the Smiths,
even Pippins
bake in the trees.

True, and of course, necessarily we're naïve.
It's hard—
hard for the precious
not to be.

Given ambition
we're shown the trajectories, rainbows
millimeters at a time.

This God grants us
its ruptures, nostalgics, the spell's
full monty as ground
to cover.

From where He watches

we zoom—

Drought pursues spring.

July waking
to its fang dry-mouthed.
All it knows
is the kindling fact that June
provoked it.

A patch of land,
a mineral, a cinder
can make a farmer its mark.

My zoom travels light as a sheered-off
curve. Whatever soul
I had is safe.
God stashed it—
as the deal

goes—with bits of Paradise
under the hill long ago.

Having a God I don't need
memory to remind me
something waits.

   * Chief

On the desert, passion
was chief
among resources:
                desire
meaning to endure.

To us it proved

worth in a soul
wrestling from a sky, the butte
in outcome
as opposed to air,

spirit
assuming it could dig.

Watching the day begin
once more, I realize, it was a glint
from Pan Lake
that provoked me.
                    Imagine
existing years like that
in between basin and sky.

Sure, I bought.
Distance would never abandon its pilgrim.

Seeing days stack towards sunset
behind Knuckle Ridge, I get
that I fell
for silver, counting

mesmerized,
same high
                suspended, counting
behind the trees.

   * Scrubland

If you put an ear to the ground
you can hear
beetles mating ahead of time.

Though you made it
through winter, by spring

you know you're a newcomer.
You work for mosquitoes.

Later, God says
you'll work for dough, largesse
of my great Second hand.

Bugs evanesce
too soon to learn of my First—
and how I lay
its promise—
on your knobby head with a weight
like gold.

   * Harvest Photograph

We climb up
the tapering ladders
into the trees.

Midges strain
to carry atoms, mere
pixels of apples.

Glazes outline the rows
which then glue us
four-square.
                From where God sits,
we're small enough

to fit a tradition
sawed in half.
              This one reveals
us tying limbs, robbing the branches—

Are we for sale?

It's hard to tell time-wise of the sliced
and remote
              whose gloves flicker,
and where browned dots deface
expression. We heap
our bushels with scarlet
droplets.

Days between summer and winter,
He sighs at the tipping point:

crates line arterial back roads,
pool in the depots
and the Valley lays back
face up.

What a triumph
is autumn.

He removes His glasses, settles His head
in Paradise,
going where vacationers go
to sleep
one more era.

* Fruit

Fruit: plummet.
But a classic pair
bedding knowledge
with shame.

The earth dives on,
oscillating on its axis.

Under God's gaze
time spins, knitting
to clothe us,

or more the spider, wind us
in the high-hum
silks that gum our skins.

Harvest tacks
to harvest, fall
to fall, one to another,
and back, adhering
for Him a layered globe.

* Early Market

The market looms.
The Southern Steeps of
Poker Range are constant,

backsides to us.

I believe what I see.
Why argue with the given.

The benches roll, corn-rowed, knotted
in calico squares.

I'm easy
to mesmerize.
Beeswax glows by the bed.
My breasts are brown
where your hand climbs.

But in fact, the path is leading
right to us,
and coming fast, aiming
straight I realize, from the heart-shaped
head of an arrow's tip.

Why must there be only one God?

　　* More, It's

Its nudge shows
the sunshine

pulling the frame
of its edges, crossing
the sheets
　　　　　each day, every day, more—

Like a snail
it sucks after the poke of its horn.

When trees blossom, ants nurse gusty aphids.

When the red oak develops acorns
and likewise the chestnut,
nuts—

I take up the rake
to rake beside you
like you beside me.
We labor
collecting the fall
as compensation,
                    and once debited,
taxed,
the surplus—
heavy enough to roll us past
winter, beyond the horizon
moving with it
                    in tandem.

Soon evidence ripens
enough to make itself
palpable—as if backed,
                    we're destined.

And by the same pace, same
logic as speed—
                    chosen.

A Reserved Attitude, Perhaps Victorian

The relation
between delphinium and larkspur
is conservative: wild petals
bred tighter
grander
distinguishes the cultivated

from scree thing. Still

some rough material
between them stays the same
even after a peak's been reached
and the garden reverts
to scruff.

While the visiting naturalist champions
the indigenous
                    and downtrodden,
and I'm grateful,
some people might also like to be Her, expectant
distiller of blue
before the decline, so carefree
she could tease
the pretensions of old formalities—
and righteous.

Delphinium, Speaking from the Frontier

Put indelicately
I was born
        a beauty.

Pretty child to cloudless spring
to elegant
legend. You may wonder

why I use past tense:
We know that's what beauty will be— recalled,

taken back.

It's in God's hands,
His surmise,
          purview and what-not—
gone.

Some think
I'm less attractive now
that I have lost
Him, less
forthcoming
than is modest—

Less imaginative perhaps—yet
it seems, a mind
this loose grows roomier, more
sky-like—

Since I've lived here
I have been learning
not to say, *Don't mention it.*

When people use the customary
Thank you, they expect, *You are welcome*
(come on in—)

I try
to say*, Sorry*
as opposed to *Pardon*

                  as my sisters said,
my sisters and I, the girls and I—said.

On the desert beauty bleaches
more purely
            where I'm no longer
the stranger
who makes the mistakes,
but kin,

an applause
of air, acquainted and delighted, with you.

Promise

You won't be lost
Dear, you'll be cast—

ground
          not heir.
Medium, not meaning.

Roiling up from the Pacific
and careening south, powerful winds
will scour spring, drive
snows in winter

but the ground will receive
you, its own—
and provide in depth, a plush
mulch to accept you, storied layers
and leaves.

This may seem to distant societies
and their anthropologists
like marriage by contract,
forced—
for all its calm appearance of commune,

delimbed—
passion converted to narrative, like fidelity
to context,
choice
to absence: effectively, dependency
or nothing.

Either way, expect to be
the means to a cycle
of beginnings and ends,
                    the currency of cause
and effect, shamanistic
bones, Dear, like mine, among the shards.

Far ahead from that,
what will they, pausing, see
searching the presumed-upon
dirt—
a valley's isotopic
measure of existence—used, fallen,
crushed to pigments.

For now, though, My dear and so
hopeful child, I expect
you'll find the questions fused

in the animating music
of nearby mountains, dust singing
and clapping along,

everyday coerced, beguiled—everyday
Easter.

Seven Candles

When I count stitches
no daughter
of mine has married a farmer.

Even as a child
learning to knit
my first audience
adored me. Seven aunts
all round to position
the needles.

I've been instructing ever since.
When I count
stitches, God holds His breath.
Then I am light,
a small summer cloud, agleam
by His Grace, His fist and scepter.

Cutting to the Lateral

It takes a God
   to recognize
   each tree, kame on kame,
   as valid—
       as right
row by row, rut by rut
tilled by pattern. We prune
the orchard—each limb
hard-cut to forthcoming

each, as the suckers fall, supplicant
by shape, lost
to shape.
   From Kettle Summit who
wouldn't believe

that it is God
who aligns with the whirling crowns
of lobbed limbs.
Rapt—the ones who spin.

Though don't
when you're powerless—
stand in their sight-lines.

Theirs is a direct
transmission.

Instead, I pile the slash
every other end of the rows.

Easy to relate to cuttings,

the amateurs
to meaning, phantoms of

geometry.
               They still provide
smoke to seed the clouds,
flavor the grill, dry
new meat
from the hills, trout from the stream.

Apex

From its climax—
the moment—a shell
breaks—
giving itself the proteins to select
its advance.

As if there were a track

that totters
like a balancing plank
across one platform.

The long end
is awkward and heavy
lifting the family preference.

As subordinate
to heir, it scrawls
in the dirt, an ample
underlying commentary.

I maintain my belief, however
in the power of commentary.

Speckled Fritillaries

1

Hang on, understand—

your father

then your mother will die.
I speak for the God of precedents.

You can flutter
elevating yourself, reaching after them—

or retract
on your boulder
but they take their deaths with them.
Backs turned, they read
the morning papers in heaven.

Without it's call
you'd suck the earth to sand, past rock.
You'd eat the core.

2

He says you can't escape Him.
It is He—modelling
His voice
on the touch of a finger
and oversizing it: as everywhere
as the summer dawn

hyper-extended.
He's tireless, the linear

resolve. He explains, O,
flittering, He's the tension
in coil, dynamic
in spring, a positive

God. Harboring His own
initiative,
             like any good boundary
He introduces and prohibits.

      3

Captivities of, millimeters
of minute

heart beats—
              pressure
under the wings
or spotted
             on a bush.   I order the count

and the result is
                 elegance.
It stitches of flight, numeric
lace.
      being the zeros
in sum,
         place holders,
wingy lapses
              in flutter,

you exist and you don't.

71

If not subsequence, pale butterflies,
you contribute,
whirr,
        ash, broom.
You invite—
            no, unleash,

                        seize,

pin, crumble.

Delphinium Speaks with Larkspur

No use believing the soul
is more than a shell
just like its God.

Others dear
won't mention this
as a shell is a fragile thing.

The straight up blue
of a zenith calls us
to correlate, resonate
with heaven's azure,
its thinning noon spur—
the sustenance
                    that floats us
by sheer right of extension.

Thus I asked Him—
on your behalf—what He gains
bending over us
between sky and earth
as if to traffic
the overall.

And for you, lark, I pushed on:
Why capitalize, Father?

When endless heaven compels
us enough
why intercede?

Why make us His
raw

        sudden vessels
whose indigo
moments running
through a petal's membranes
bursting—

add music
to His ears,
            ringing
His where-with-all
                        linking
value with increase?

We are close, lark, me taller,
brighter, louder,
but still we share a bond,
ruffling our blues in the wind,
then closing
when the sun sets behind the Sawtooths.

Inside His robe
wide and sheltering
as a warehouse, He fills
the withholding cold of the void
all night,
            stacking inventory,
tabulating miles
and accounting for blades of grass
living and dying,
bushels of hay,
                granting
each commodity, a soul.

Which through His largesse, then circulates.

74

Larkspur Addressing Delphinium

Gazing across the habitat,
I am that slighter blue
minute that aspires
to your fully celestial hour.

Between larkspur and
delphinium
                  there's been a relapse.
We watched your apex
together on either side
of a generation
degenerate.

Now most retro
of a species, I return to sun
on the slopes of the gap,
hoping to link
my feral self, my fiber
and being, to your golden age.

When amplified in you,
how great by extension I became,
and by weight, my memory expanded

inviting God to insert Himself
into my longing,
a God too canny, kind, to say
He tips the earth
to keep me running.

Delphinium/ Larkspur

In our petals we
sense that
gravity as high as Him has ceased,

but out of delicacy,

spare him the knowledge
that beyond the warm sun and
its bestowals,

beyond consequences,

numerical odds, and outside
all edges,
let alone cracks,

beyond rate, and keep, and promise
and size,
    beyond any resurrectible
momento, glomming particle,
granule, anti-or otherwise,
He has no need for air.

Summer Evening

When day ends
when darkness begins
where is God?

The earth is not a ball

not an emigrant rolling east,
or is it? In God's hands
the planet
rounds as He pushes it away.

Arguments of dawn, pageants of dusks
He reminds one—

of the reaches
required to
to refigure embrace,

rotes of
          the spatial need
for wrap-up,

a similar's
need
      bringing home closure—
space
        cradling the spun,

                              space
freckled
with tinted debris, that—would be
some father
some mother.

Out gleeful
on the great black lawn
brothers, sisters, relations of all sparkle
seek configurations
in grand tow
to watchers here.

Pink, icy,
acid-toothed,
ochred,
          icteroid.

Red-Tail Basin

* Hut

The adobe, the hut.

Habit makes itself
cozy,
        seeking
the early in pleasure.

Model.
Then law.

Such a law on sweetness concentrated it:

sugar crystal
growing on a string-thing. Cutting—

the way
        it ruled: little shucks
and carved whistle.

And piercing
its tune, straight to the tooth.

* Wall

    Then nothing convinced
like a wall, any
old mother wall. Nothing provided a sturdier
purpose
        for thought.
The wall must kick free

its young.
            Had to.
They would crowd the brain with their bubbling.

    * Illustration

perhaps a doodle of Van Gogh's orchard,
with inserted child waving from a branch

    * Pleated Stretches of Heritage Delicious

Into the new days
both Red and Yellow
Delicious stand
4-square
marking greater depths
to the smack
of clean limbs, primed buds

nicked at their stems,
down rows
of sandstone canyons
allowing what's red to amend
itself pink
ruffled white in the return.

    * Gift

Eden-time in the red
predefinitions, you are
still a miracle—

accessory to
                consequence, not
yet interfering,
unjudged and uncondemning,

little
paisley-tail absorbed
in the progression—
but not yet perp.

    * Cloudless Skies

The grove of apple trees scooped
itself from darkness
to spring,

surging up in a prefix of light and
summer. It was here
that I sometimes nudged you by slithering,
and more often by dangling.

You remember the fork in the limbs.
I compelled you
while answering
                to no one.
And it wasn't
as if hunger
hadn't borne itself too
out of nowhere, while the skin of scarlet
apples slanted your way
a throng of white lights.
Come in. Come in,
a fleck said.

You bit.

Some call it matricide
this siding with hunger,

                  choosing promise

to lead and protect you
(with His beard, and shiny hair).
But you already knew
the Goddess of course
was already dead.

Wide-angle

Banks of clouds—
though creeping—and one sky
but cumulative: skies borrowing from one another
passage.

Smoke
threading vines
from neighborhood stoves
blend with spring mountain
burns

but above all, smoke gears us

with the bees
to sleepwalk the hard stuff.

We separate
honey from honey.

And from the cavity of a hive,

ardency
        that morphs
substance from substance,
extracting
gold honey, stupor of
apple mead, eventually a person

stolen
or pillaged

from the side of the road as soon
as a four-poster bed,

may be left to the bones
that clasp an embrace,

and everything
like grass
cut ahead of summer's real wild fires
blows away.

No iron
in the girders, no girders
hefting the government
Forkville Bridge.
Which might've led back.
That was the plan.

Throat

As the conversation struggles
God clears his final throat:

Destiny—
                    when frozen to an apple
                    or met by blood
                    red with iron—will stand up

and circulate
shaped like a Stetson, or wafer.

As He describes it, I picture
a lazy-hazy twirling
lasso
        hanging
on air
a fiery lozenge of
seasons

            ratio-ed
between the sun and earth's opposing
pulls.

From a grown girl's point of view
how sad is this, at home
on a Saturday night

still talking politics.

Ledger

How sentimental
could gravity make a person?
Year after year
                    I anticipated
from stubs and brown petals,
nubbins
            waxing in clusters
signaling withdrawal: *yes* from

no to *yes* again, so slowly
we could feel our way,
extracting one size from another,

deep russet from russet, cool
from cold.
            I became
the conversion

tracking the magnetic

in claim, the earth's own
reliance on, weight and dependence
on sequence.

From where God sat, clouds
left a trail,

glints of sand cast a line
we could lift
            on His behalf

and apply

to border, to country
pushed by the winded
                    redoubling
quickening development
                         leading
via boundary
to region to recoil, the swift
autonomic
path from retaliation
full circle

to nation,
           one

whose system of interplay
fulcrummed on zero.

Cellar

You have my blessing
    God said
to see yourselves

all together
in the vivant tableau's sliced
embrace.

Be cornucopian.
              Be of
the barrel, cloth, fiddle.

Doing the math
where G=green, R=red or shades
of the ruddy family,
           B=tan=also depth then

$$(G)_0 \times G + R - (Y)_1 + (Y)_7 \times B \times B/_B = BGR$$

(Y* *pegged to the earth)

Test it:

G—gravity B—body R—rise.

Or if October darkness were a legend
we've settled

as into the hollow under the spruce root.

Frenzy, release—

those things risked
above the frozen barkdust
collide where tension bonds the triumphant
and the industriously
bleeding, well-meaning
naked.

Down here, we could constitute
a tubful of wintering
jonagolds,
          chill
holding fragrance,
             and this,
our moment, our cradle

and fizz:
         dreaming
musk of bruised honey
in a was
and will be, end-stop.

His arm
I have to say, rounds
His commitment, pulling us—
bloated, urgent—in.

Where does a mind go?
stalled with the flesh
in a Dutch still life
but catabolic?

IV

Alibi Pass

Then it so happened
once upon one daybreak,
the orchard stood
chewed—

spit out. You could call it, the cottony
touchez's
            of a final authority,

what He held over us:
the impenetrable difference
of next—

It mimicked the gate

gaping still
from its hinge
and creaking like geese flying
toward fall,
            heading north,
then west, peeling
like a cap of skin.

Curve

That dawn my mind
walked itself to the steppe's edge to curve
with the earth

plunging its weight forward: Day—

one obliged to hang
and inhabit
catastrophe, a place already

heavily decorated

with charms—
prayers, rocks, figurines.
I'm sure I'd have chosen to argue
forever inside light's spreading version
of presto

as it burned into hours.
How to align
with power?

How to make moments
add up

correctly. I observed the tip
and induction where two,
the future and past,
came together.
How to farm inside the politics

where one gave way to the mandate
of the other, then

together
pressed us, drove us
toward openings and widenings, an overhead vision

plush as a robe's lining,
shepherded us
while all along the steep course, we were carted.

When god says, meet me,
now, I know I'm going down.

A bell
ringing the intervals.

Under Birdwoman Glacier

Bee crates lined the orchard aisles,
cracked, warping some,
grass bunching round
the bottom slats: there would be
gain:
          we walked it—

choosing our way
through July's heat

nearly so parched
as to bake ourselves sand
into glass:
                glass all yesterday,
all tomorrow,
and the bees whisked into flight.

Zippered hoods, slats of honeycomb, the daily
homespun a priori
of hand
          in hand—

Pollen caught in the mesh,
the nylon haze, salt of
so many veils
to penetrate
back, witnessing

the gold corridor of cottonwoods
that buckled up from the banks,

altered the ditch
to expanse.

In time
           or not—it became a beginning.
An orchard is not just a tease.
It puts out.

Inside the Horizon

My heart wasn't good
at conducting
an argument, nor at nurturing
a point, though eventually, and this took
a while, I understood
what God was trying hard to tell me—

that He needed to teach me:

No Pain/No Gain.

Something like shoulder—
speed—
            dust,

though glamorous dust

that sparkles with the vermeil
of His signature
                    clouds
banked in dusk.

Skew

Usually it's in the spare
moment that a question comes curling along

like a disease in the path.
                              Can it skew
a story?   So many

diseases, plunging
temperatures, or sunspots
happy to disrupt the patterns presumed in a leaf.

The leaf shrivels, tears
from its stem.

When a story tears
(scribble of lightning)

there's a cracking flash,

the sky splits
and the backdrop behind the sky is revealed—
chaos
(you've seen it)
now and from here on out.

Weathered Shed

Some days, the past procrastinates
like the guest who shows
no sign of leaving—

or the illness that arrives too early
rejoicing
to have a voice

so that the hills overhear
dead grass

brown, happy to be final,
to beat its own
odds, and before, by all bets, snow

takes over,
and then blowing, resnows,

secondary—or in the aspen sense,
daughterly, one white
is any other.

The past
would upend any given order.

Snuffed—
          why not.

Arial Weave

An orchard steadies the mind.
Is kind that way.

I appreciate
kindness so inadvertent, kindness

unmeant, yet
hearkening back as an orchard does

to ancient groves: valley in blossom,
mountain peaks snow-veined.

Suckers around trunks tap that
authority, reconcile old

with fresh, to sanction place
historical, as if

in history a person exists
one to another,

social, however
it can be arranged.

Ditch

Often when God isn't looking,
I pretend I check
the orchards' irrigation,
but in a different world,

one where gravity holds
my feet lightly
kicking through cherry leaves.
The quack grass bends back,
but in a back that reminds my ankles
they tramp—
rubbed.

It's the ground's way to give
my soles
turf, and the spring, thereof. Purple
thistle bristles
in the lower corner of the field.
Yet its feathery brush lingers.

Like other ragged
late-blooming undergrowth united
at the fenceposts,
independents
in the New World sense
it invites me
when crossing the field to remember

I don't need bulk
or luck, sweat

or muscles as beautiful as Adam's
(with whom God is often distracted)
to belong to the field.

Season of Corn Snow

The trees float
hanks of frost
            which gusts
kick up as second snow.

If nothing else
the conditioned understand

transaction.
From a tall window

I see it clinch
posterity, inflate,
pause, exhale—

and again, as resale
or scrap.
It's true that
love can dissolve

can, unlike its carriers, reverse,
re-separate, and backwards,
disperse.

So bare, so thin
down there
the winter trees shudder.

Too much silence and you'll hear
My neutrality. Barren
reduces to bare; bare clacks
on bare.

Caterpillars

So much
depends on not knowing.
Like a spell.

Like the tension
between headlong and
ground.
      Dedication
to dedication, a calling

was like that, calling
ahead. You were meant
to feel

the wind's vigor
on your face.
And to risk—that was the currency

that promised
not to cash-in, deflate or go missing.

How to connect
without the valuable
at stake between us?

Reveille

The lakes roll
under the ice, heat
taken to heart, released

or forsaken—why

is the model the same?

The river breaks.
Nothing grows.
No one skates in March.

Survival: it's here too
with its inbred

nearly patrician—aversive
endurance.
                    For all its power-out-of-here
flashback can't compete
with dawn

whose fingers streak the valley,
comb green pines still upwardly
alchemical.
They ignite for even the disabused.

About the Author

Ann Douglas' first book of poems, *After*, won the Seattle/King County Manuscript Award and was positively reviewed in Publishers' Weekly. She is a Squaw Valley Writers' Community member, and has benefited from residencies at Yaddow, Ragdale, and the Sitka Artist in Residence Program. She holds an MFA from Columbia University, and works in Washington State as a psychotherapist in private practice.